SPOTTER'S GUIDE TO
THE SEASHORE

Su

Illustrated by John Barber

Designed by Russell Punter

Edited by Susan Meredith, Sue Tarsky and Jessica Datta

Series editor: Philippa Wingate
Cover design and series designer: Laura Fearn
Cover illustration by Ian Jackson

Consultants: Margaret Rostron, Christopher Humphries, Ian Tittley, Shirley Stone, Paul Cornelius, Kathie Way, Ailsa Clark, Ray Ingle, David George, Alwyne Wheeler, Martin Sheldrick and Peter Holden

Picture acknowledgements: backgrounds - pages 1, 2-3, 4-5, 6, 7(l), 8-9, 14-15, 22-23, 24-25, 26-27, 28-29, 30-31, 32-33, 34-35, 38-39, 42-43, 46-47, 50-51, 54, 56-57, 58-62 © Digital Vision;
background - page 7(r) © Barry Davies;Eye Ubiquitous/CORBIS;
guillemot - page 9 © Digital Vision; background - page 12 © FPG/iSwoop.

First published in 2000 by Usborne Publishing Ltd, Usborne House, 83-85 Saffron Hill, London EC1N 8RT, England. www.usborne.com
Copyright © 2000, 1985, 1978 Usborne Publishing Ltd.

CONTENTS

HOW TO USE THIS BOOK

There are thousands of different animals and plants to spot on the seashore. This book shows you some of them and helps you to identify them.

Each different kind of animal or plant is called a species. The descriptions next to each picture tell you what details to look for, where you are likely to find the species and how big it might be.

KEEPING A RECORD

Next to each picture is an empty circle. Whenever you spot a species for the first time, you can put a tick in the circle.

You can also fill in the scorecard at the back of the book, to give yourself a score for each species spotted. A common species scores 5 points and a very rare one is worth 25 points.

There are thousands of species of bird. The great black-backed gull is one of them.

WHAT LIVES WHERE?

The animals and plants in this book can be found in the areas shown in yellow on this map. A few of the species described may be very rare where you live. These species may be common in other European countries, though, so you will have a chance to spot them if you go abroad.

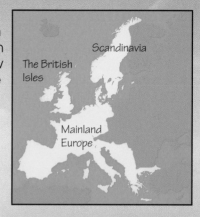

Scandinavia

The British Isles

Mainland Europe

WHERE TO LOOK

There are four main kinds of beach: rocky, sandy, muddy and shingle. You will find different species on each, although just a few can live on all kinds of beach. You can also find seashore life, especially birds and plants, on saltmarshes and in estuaries.

ROCKY SHORES

Rocky shores are the ideal place for many plants and animals to live. Look among the rocks for shells and seaweeds, and in rock pools for fish, crabs, starfish and sea anemones.

SANDY AND MUDDY SHORES

Both sandy and muddy shores are good places to watch wading birds and to look for the burrowing crabs, shellfish and worms which they feed on.

SHINGLE SHORES

Little can grow on a shingle beach because the pebbles are always being moved by the sea and don't hold water when the tide is out. Look for seaweeds and empty shells washed ashore.

TIDES

The sea moves up and down the beach twice in every 24 hours, so there are two high tides (when the sea reaches its highest level) and two low tides (when it reaches its lowest point).

To live between high and low tide levels, animals and plants must be able to withstand the waves and currents. They must also be able to survive periods both in and out of the water.

The lower shore is uncovered only at low tide. Lots of plants and animals live here.

The upper shore is underwater only at high tide. Few species live here but some survive attached to rocks when the tide goes out.

Sea

Lower shore

Middle shore

Upper shore

The middle shore is underwater about half the time. Many species live here.

KEEPING SAFE

Before you go onto a beach, check that it is safe. Look for warning signs and flags, and check the times of the tides so you don't get stranded. You will find the times in the local paper, at the library, or at the lifeguards' or harbour master's office.

Don't eat anything you find on the beach; even if it is an edible species, it may well be polluted.

Beware of scrapes from barnacles, stings from spiny animals and nips from crabs. Many biologists wear latex gloves for handling finds.

CONSERVATION

Seashore life is under threat from many types of pollution. Pollutants are dumped in the sea by ships and washed into it from rivers; sewage is pumped into it and litter is left by tourists.

Visit the Web sites listed on page 57 if you want to find out more about pollution and what can be done to combat it.

This guillemot has been covered in oil spilled from a tanker.

WHAT YOU CAN DO

When you are looking at animals and plants, try to disturb them as little as possible. If you move something to have a look at it, handle it very gently and put it back where you found it. Many species cannot survive out of sea water, so put them in a container of sea water to have a good look at them.

If you move rocks or stones to look under them, always put them back in position. You might like to collect a few shells, but make sure they are empty and don't still have a living creature inside. Don't pick flowers, and don't take anything at all from a nature reserve - it is against the law. Don't leave litter.

MEASURING YOUR FINDS

The animals and plants in this book are not drawn to scale, but the descriptions next to the pictures tell you their size. Here you can see how they are measured. Some species are measured differently from others. For example, crabs are measured without their claws, and sponges may be measured lengthways or widthways.

Measuring species will help you to identify them, but remember that young ones will be smaller than fully grown ones.

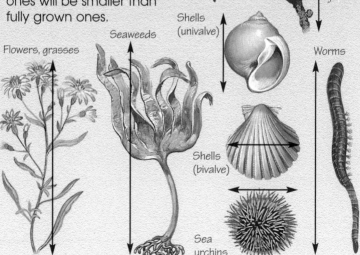

Starfish

Sea slugs

Corals

Flowers, grasses

Seaweeds

Shells (univalve)

Shells (bivalve)

Worms

Sea urchins

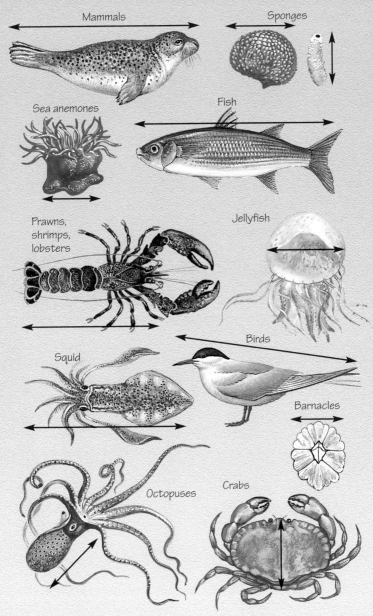

Mammals

Sponges

Sea anemones

Fish

Prawns, shrimps, lobsters

Jellyfish

Birds

Squid

Barnacles

Octopuses

Crabs

11

WHAT TO TAKE

You might like to take some equipment with you when you go spotting. Here are some of the most useful things:

- fishing net for exploring rock pools
- bucket or box to put finds in while you look at them
- magnifying glass for looking at small animals and plants
- binoculars for watching birds, seals or dolphins
- small trowel for digging in the sand
- sieve for sifting sand to find animals buried in it

- tape measure to help you identify finds by their size
- notebook, pen and pencils to record what you find
- plastic bags for shells and pebbles
- this book

You can keep a record of the species you find by making a note of the date and place where you spotted them, and by doing a sketch.

Common starfish

Date: 5 July
Place: Gull Bay

FLOWERS AND GRASSES

Look for flowers on shingle and sandy beaches, cliffs, dunes and saltmarshes. To identify them, notice the overall shape of the plants and their leaves too.

➡ YELLOW HORNED POPPY
Called horned because of the long green pods which appear in summer. Flowers June-Sept. Shingle beaches. Up to 1m.

Pod

◀ SEA KALE
Grows in clumps on shingle. Broad, fleshy leaves have crinkly edges. Flowers June-August. Up to 1m.

➡ GOLDEN SAMPHIRE
Sturdy plant with shiny, fleshy leaves. Often grows in large clumps on saltmarshes, shingle and cliffs. Flowers in autumn. 60cm.

◀ SEA SANDWORT
Common creeping plant on loose sand and shingle. Helps to stop sand drifting. Flowers May-August. 30cm.

13

FLOWERS AND GRASSES

← SEA HOLLY
Prickly plant with clusters of tiny flowers, which attract butterflies. Its thick leaves turn white in winter. Sand and shingle. Up to 50cm.

➡ SEA WORMWOOD (left)
Strong-smelling plant. Leaves are downy and greyish green. Grows above high tide level in estuaries. Up to 50cm.

➡ SEA PURSLANE (middle)
Grows on edges of deep channels in saltmarshes. Flowers June-Oct. 60cm.

➡ MARRAM GRASS (right)
Common on sand dunes. Its long roots and leaves trap sand and stop it blowing away. Flowers July-August. Up to 1.2m.

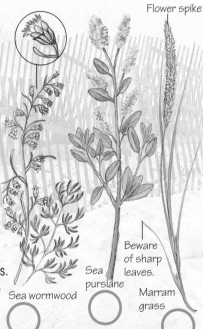

Flower spike

Beware of sharp leaves.

Sea purslane

Sea wormwood

Marram grass

← SEA BINDWEED
Trailing plant with thick, shiny leaves. Can be seen on sand dunes and sometimes on shingle. Flowers June-Sept.

➡ ANNUAL SEABLITE

May grow along the ground or upright. Fleshy leaves. On saltmarshes in areas of bare mud. 20cm.

Downy leaves

Sea milkwort

Sea arrowgrass

⬅ SEA MILKWORT (left)

Creeping plant that spreads over grassy saltmarshes. Flowers June-August.

⬅ SEA ARROWGRASS (right)

Tough plant with flat, sharp leaves. Flowers May-Sept. Grassy saltmarshes. 15-50cm.

➡ SEA LAVENDER (left)

Tough, woody plant with leaves in a clump near the ground. Muddy saltmarshes. Flowers July-Sept. Up to 40cm.

➡ SEA ASTER (right)

Flowers in late summer, with lilac or white petals. Saltmarshes. Up to 1m.

Sea lavender

Sea aster

FLOWERS AND GRASSES

➡ THRIFT or SEA PINK (left)
Grows in thick, cushiony tufts on rocky cliffs. Flowers March-Sept. 15cm.

➡ SEA MAYWEED (right)
May be creeping or upright. Feathery leaves. Daisy-like flowers. Grows on cliffs. Up to 60cm.

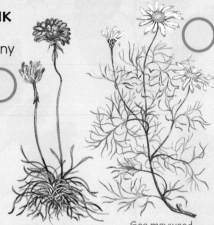

Thrift or Sea pink   Sea mayweed

Seed pods

⬅ BIRD'S FOOT TREFOIL
Bright yellow flowers streaked with red. Seed pods split and curl when ripe to release seeds. Grassy banks and cliffs. 10cm.

➡ BUCKSHORN PLANTAIN (right)
Hairy leaves grow from a point close to the ground. Look on gravel near the sea. Spikes of flowers May-Oct. 10cm.

➡ SEA CAMPION (left)
Common on cliffs and shingle beaches. Spreads to form cushions. Flowers June-August. 20cm.

Flower spike

Sea campion   Buckshorn plantain

SEAWEEDS

Rocky shores are the best places to look for seaweeds.
Some can live both in and out of the water, as the tide
comes in and goes out.

➡ GUT LAVER (left)
Tube-like fronds do not
branch. May cover pools on
upper shore and in estuaries.
Very common. 20cm.

➡ SEA LETTUCE (right)
Common on rocky shores
at middle and lower levels.
Fronds become dark green
with age. 20cm.

Gut laver

Sea lettuce

Frond

Frond

Disc

⬅ MERMAID'S CUP
Disc shape on thin stalk
made up of many tiny
segments pressed close
together. On rocks in
sheltered bays.

➡ BRYOPSIS (left)
Looks shiny. Found on steep
sides of rock pools on middle
and lower shore. 7.5cm.

Male plant -
female is darker

Sea chain

➡ SEA CHAIN (right)
Feels hard and brittle because it
is covered with lime. Shallow
water in sheltered bays.
Mediterranean. 15cm.

Bryopsis

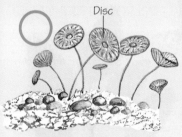

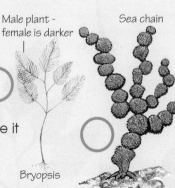

SEAWEEDS

➡ BLADDER WRACK
Pairs of air bladders help to keep plant upright in water. Fixed to rocks by large root-like holdfast. Up to 60cm.

Air bladder

⬇ KNOTTED WRACK
Stem is round near holdfast, flat further up. Strap-like fronds. On sheltered rocks of middle shore. Up to 1m.

Tufts of red seaweed

Air bladder

⬇ OARWEED
Wide blade divides into strap-like fronds. On rocks in shallow water. 1.5m.

Holdfast

Frond

Blade

Holdfast

⬇ SARGASSO WEED
Bushy, with branching stem. Leafy fronds. Shallow water in Mediterranean. Up to 2m.

Air bladder

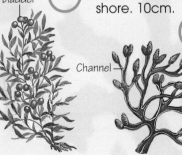

⬇ CHANNELLED WRACK
Frond edges curve in to form channels. Look on rocks on upper shore. 10cm.

Channel

➤ PHYMATOLITHON

Some red seaweeds, like this one, have a hard coating of lime. It forms a crust in patches on rocks and stones on middle and lower shore.

◄ LAVER

Bumpy fronds are usually attached at one point. On sand-covered stones, on middle to lower shore. On rocks on upper shore. 15cm.

➤ PLOCAMIUM

Small tufted plant with finely-divided fronds. Feathery tips only grow on one side of each branch. In shallow water or washed ashore. 15-20cm.

Narrow form   Broad form

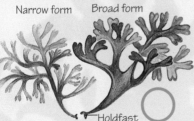

Holdfast

◄ IRISH MOSS

Two forms, broad and narrow. Found on rocks on middle and lower shore. Look for the small, disc-shaped holdfast. 15cm.

➤ SEA OAK

Fronds shaped like oak leaves, with markings like veins. Grows on lower shore rocks, in pools and on stalks of large brown seaweeds. 20cm.

Stalk of brown seaweed

19

SPONGES

Most sponges are found on the lower shore, usually on rocks. They look like plants but are really animals.

◄ SCYPHA CILIATA
Shaggy, upright tube, often with fringed top. Lives singly or in clusters in damp, shady places. On stones or among seaweed. Up to 12cm long.

◄ SEA ORANGE
Round, orange sponge. Surface is grooved. In shallow water but more often seen offshore. Up to 7cm across.

▼ BREAD SPONGE
Crumbles when handled. Many different shapes, and varies from green to yellow. On rocks, shells and seaweed holdfasts. Middle and lower shores. 10cm across.

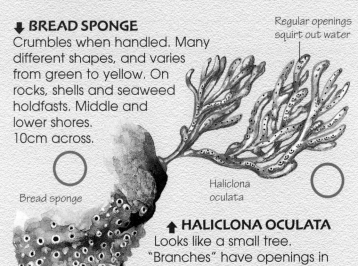

Regular openings squirt out water

Bread sponge

Haliclona oculata

▲ HALICLONA OCULATA
Looks like a small tree. "Branches" have openings in them. On lower shores in fast currents and in estuaries with muddy gravel. Up to 16cm long.

CORALS

Corals are made up of many tiny animals, called polyps. Their outer skeletons join together to form a large colony which looks like a plant.

➡ PRECIOUS CORAL
Lives in deep water in the Mediterranean. Rare. 50cm.

➡ CUP CORAL
There is one animal in each cup-shaped skeleton. On rocks of lower shore. 3cm.

Precious coral

Cup coral

Sea fan

Dead man's fingers

⬆ DEAD MAN'S FINGERS
Lives in chunky, hand-shaped colonies. May be white, pink or yellow. Offshore, but washed up after storms. 20cm.

⬆ SEA FAN
Notice individual white animals on branches of colony. Seen on rocks in clear water, or washed ashore. 50cm.

SEA ANEMONES

These flower-like animals use their tentacles to capture food. When they are not underwater, their tentacles are drawn in.

➡ BEADLET ANEMONE
Red or green with a blue spot below each tentacle and a thin blue line round the base. Common in rock pools. 3cm.

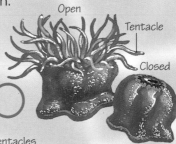

Open

Tentacle

Closed

Feathery tentacles

⬅ PLUMOSE ANEMONE
May be orange or white. Often seen on pier supports, just below water surface. 7cm.

➡ SNAKELOCKS ANEMONE
Can be grey or greenish. The sticky tentacles shrink when touched but do not disappear. Rocky shores, sometimes on oarweed. 8cm.

Open

Closed

⬅ WARTLET ANEMONE
Body varies from green to red, with six rows of white warts. Striped tentacles. In lower shore rock pools and crevices. 4cm.

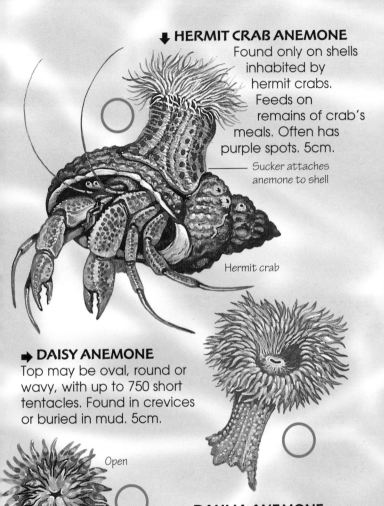

↓ HERMIT CRAB ANEMONE

Found only on shells inhabited by hermit crabs. Feeds on remains of crab's meals. Often has purple spots. 5cm.

Sucker attaches anemone to shell

Hermit crab

➡ DAISY ANEMONE

Top may be oval, round or wavy, with up to 750 short tentacles. Found in crevices or buried in mud. 5cm.

Open

⬅ DAHLIA ANEMONE

Colours vary. Warty body often covered with bits of shell, making it hard to spot in rock pools. 8cm.

Closed

23

FISH

Look at the shape of a fish's body, its
fins, and whether or not it has spines on
its back. Try spotting fish in rock pools.

➡ SHORE CLINGFISH
Clings to rocks with sucker. In
pools, on seaweed-covered
lower shores. Both parents
guard golden eggs. 6.5cm.

Sucker

⬅ SHORE ROCKLING
Rocky shores, in pools
and shallow water.
·Under stones· and
seaweed. Finds food with
its three long barbels. 27cm.

Barbel

➡ SCORPION FISH
Spines on fin and gill covers
are venomous, so do not
touch them. Hides in
seaweed in shallow water
and rock pools. 15cm.

Venomous spine

⬅ SEA STICKLEBACK
Lives among seaweeds in
shallow water on rocky,
sandy and muddy shores.
Builds nest of seaweed
where its eggs hatch. 16cm.

➡ CORKWING WRASSE
Eats animals with shells,
which it crushes with its
strong teeth. In weedy
pools. Colour varies. 26cm.

← MONTAGU'S BLENNY
Blennies do not have scales. This one lives in bare-sided rock pools. Eats acorn barnacles (see page 44). 8cm.

→ TOMPOT BLENNY
Lives mainly below low tide mark in rock crevices. Male guards eggs, which are laid in small cracks in rock. 30cm.

← BUTTERFISH
Slippery body is flattened sideways. Common among rocks, under seaweed and stones on all kinds of shore. Lays eggs in winter. 25cm.

→ ROCK GOBY
Lives on rocky shores in pools and shallow water, under stones or among seaweed. Lays its eggs under flat stones. 12cm.

← WORM PIPEFISH
Hides among brown seaweeds, mostly on rocky shores. Male carries eggs under its body until they hatch. 15cm.

25

FISH

➡ STARGAZER
Lies buried in sand with only its eyes showing. Feeds on small crabs and fish. Has two venomous spines. Mediterranean. 25cm.

Venomous spine

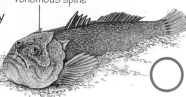

⬅ SAND GOBY
Like all gobies, has a sucker on underside. Notice dark spots on dorsal fin and blotches on sides. In shoals on sand in shallow water. 9cm.

Dorsal fin

➡ SAND EEL
Swims in large shoals in shallow water. Burrows into sand if alarmed. Often eaten by other fish. 20cm.

⬅ DAB
Common on sandy and gravelly bottoms, where its colour acts as a camouflage. Feeds on animals with shells, and on worms. 25cm.

➡ WEEVER
Has very venomous spines. Shuffle your feet when paddling to avoid treading on it. Lies buried in sand in shallow water. 14cm.

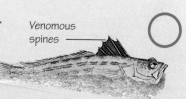
Venomous spines

← SAND-SMELT
Usually seen near surface of water, swimming in large shoals over sandy bottom. Lays eggs on seaweed. Notice dark band on side. 15cm.

→ THICK-LIPPED GREY MULLET
Often in large shoals near the surface of the sea, but feeds on plants on mud bottoms. Very thick upper lip. 70cm.

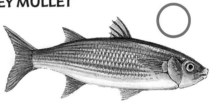

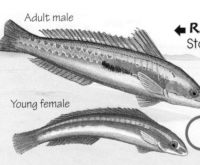

Adult male

Young female

← RAINBOW WRASSE
Starts life as female, brownish in colour. May become male, with bright colours, after a year or so. Digs into sand at night. 25cm.

→ TWO-BANDED BREAM
Marked with two dark bands. Found in small schools close to seaweed-covered rocks. Eats small animals. 30cm.

BIRDS

Look for birds on all types of beach and, in spring and early summer, nesting on cliffs.

➡ CORMORANT (left)
Nests on rocky coasts and inland. Look for the white face patch. 92cm.

➡ SHAG (right)
Most live on rocky coasts. Crest is visible only in spring. No face patch. 76cm.

Cormorant

Shag

Cormorants and shags often fly low, close to the water

Colourful beak and reddish feet in summer

⬅ PUFFIN
Nests in holes, usually on grassy cliff tops. More common in the north of Britain. Spends winter at sea. 30cm.

➡ RAZORBILL
Likes to nest in cracks in cliff, although a few may live on cliff ledges with guillemots. Spends winter at sea. 30cm.

Summer

Winter

Summer

Winter

⬅ GUILLEMOT
Large crowded colonies nest on cliff ledges, high above the sea. Guillemots spend the winter at sea. 42cm.

Pale back seen in flight

➡ CURLEW
The largest wading bird. Nests inland but visits coasts, especially estuaries, at other times. 57cm.

◀ AVOCET
Rare wader. Feeds in shallow pools. Moves its head from side to side while sifting food with upturned bill. 43cm.

➡ OYSTERCATCHER
Feeds on shellfish, which it opens with its strong bill. Seen all year round. In flocks in winter. 43cm.

Male

Female

◀ SHELDUCK
Large duck which likes sandy or muddy coasts. Often nests in old rabbit burrows. Young sometimes in flocks, guarded by a few adults. 41cm.

➡ CHOUGH
A crow which lives on high, rocky sea cliffs and in mountains. Like a jackdaw, but has red feet and red beak. 38cm.

BIRDS

← GREAT BLACK-BACKED GULL
Look for its black back and pale legs. Usually seen alone or in small numbers. Will kill and eat smaller birds. 66cm.

➡ LESSER BLACK-BACKED GULL
Although some spend the winter in Britain, most are summer visitors. Often seen inland. Dark grey back and yellow legs in summer. 53cm.

← HERRING GULL
Found near most coasts. Nests in colonies on cliffs, or sometimes on houses. Grey streaks on head in winter. 56cm.

➡ BLACK-HEADED GULL
Small gull. Dark brown head in summer; small dark blotch on head in winter. Red beak and legs all year round. Also common inland. 37cm.

Summer   Winter

← COMMON TERN
Nests in large groups on beaches and sand dunes. Notice the long wings and tail streamers in flight. Summer visitor. 34cm.

← LITTLE TERN
A summer visitor to Britain which nests in small groups on shingle beaches. Dives for fish. 24cm.

→ ROCK DOVE
Town pigeons are descended from these birds. Usually seen in small groups on sea cliffs. 33cm.

Band across top of head

Young

← RINGED PLOVER
Small, plump wader with short bill. Runs along sandy and shingle beaches, tilting over to feed. All year round in Britain. 19cm.

→ DUNLIN
Plumage varies between grey and brown. Feeds in flocks on sandy beaches. Down-curved beak. Mainly a winter visitor. 19cm.

Winter

Summer

← REDSHANK
Named after its orange-red legs. White back and hind wing edges seen in flight. Estuaries and muddy shores all year round. 28cm.

31

MAMMALS

All mammals breathe air. Seals swim with their heads above the water for air; dolphins and porpoises take it in through a blow-hole on top of their heads.

➡ MEDITERRANEAN MONK SEAL
Lives on small rocky beaches on islands. Feeds on fish. It is rare, and the only seal found in the Mediterranean. Not in Britain. 3m.

⬅ COMMON SEAL
Colour varies, but adults always spotted. Lives in herds on sandbanks and in estuaries. Fast swimmer, and can stay underwater for up to 30 minutes. 1.8m.

➡ GREY SEAL
Lives in small herds on rocky shores. Rests on land at low tide and at sunset, but also sleeps in water. Shy animal. 2.9m.

⬅ OTTER
Sometimes in sea or estuaries, but more often inland near fresh water. Swims well, with long thick tail and webbed feet. Active mainly at night. 1.25m.

Look for webbed footprints

← COMMON PORPOISE

Smaller than a dolphin, with blunt snout. Often swims near the coast, in small schools. Eats herring and other fish. 1.8m.

➡ BOTTLE-NOSED DOLPHIN

In schools of up to several hundred dolphins, often near coast. Likes swimming near boats and jumping high out of the water. 3.6m.

← COMMON DOLPHIN

Has slim body and long, narrow beak. Swims fast, up to 40kph. Playful and may jump right out of the water. In large schools. Seen around boats. 2.4m.

Beak

➡ LESSER RORQUAL

A small whale, with about 50 grooves on its throat. Feeds on drifting plants and animals. 9.1m.

Grooves

← WHITE-BEAKED DOLPHIN

May be in schools of up to 1,500 dolphins. Looks like bottle-nosed dolphin, but with shorter, whitish beak. 3m.

MOLLUSCS

These animals have a hard shell on the outside which protects their soft bodies. All the shells you find on the seashore once belonged to a mollusc. Molluscs that have two shells joined together by muscles are called bivalves.

Foot is under shell

← COMMON LIMPET
Clings to rock with muscular foot. Feeds on seaweed. Common on rocky shores. 7cm.

→ SLIPPER LIMPET
Often attached to each other in chains, with females at the bottom and males on top. Estuaries. 2.5cm.

← COMMON MUSSEL
On rocky shores and in estuaries, attached to rocks by thin threads. 1-10cm.

→ DOG WHELK
Common in rock crevices, on barnacles (see page 44). Colour depends on what food it eats. 3cm.

← COMMON PERIWINKLE
Look for it close to the sea on all kinds of shore. Feeds on seaweed. 2.5cm.

➡ COMMON CERITH

On stones, or buried in sand or mud. Hermit crabs sometimes live in empty shells. Mediterranean. 4.5cm.

⬅ DOVE SHELL

Found on rocky shores. Colour varies. Mediterranean. 4.5cm.

➡ PAINTED TOPSHELL

On rocks and under stones. Can be yellow or pink, with red stripes. 2.5cm high.

⬅ NETTED DOG WHELK

At or below low tide level on rocky shores. Likes sandy crevices. 2.5cm.

➡ SADDLE OYSTER

Sticks to rocks. Two valves look different. One is saddle-shaped. Middle and lower shore. 6cm.

⬅ FOOL'S CAP

Usually in deep water but may be attached to other shells or rocks on lower shore. 1.2cm.

MOLLUSCS

→ NUN COWRIE
Has dark spots on top of
shell. Look under stones
and in rock crevices. 1cm.

← FILE SHELL
White shell with ribs. In
rock crevices and under
stones. Mediterranean.
5cm.

Rib

→ WHITE PIDDOCK
Burrows into soft rock,
wood and firm sand.
On lower shore. 15cm.

← COMMON OYSTER
Shell shape varies and
two halves are not the
same. In shallow and
deep water. 10cm.

→ STING WINKLE
Drills a hole in oyster
shells to eat the flesh
inside. 6cm.

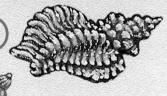

← COMMON WHELK
Very common on rocky
and sandy beaches.
Lower shore. 8cm.

➡ GREAT TOPSHELL

Usually lives in deep water but empty shells are often washed up on shore. Notice reddish zig-zag stripes. 2cm high.

◀ VARIEGATED SCALLOP

A bivalve with one "ear" twice as long as the other. Can be many different colours. Very low down on shore. 6cm.

Ear

➡ LURID COWRIE

On muddy and sandy bottoms, often in very deep water. Washed ashore in the Mediterranean. 5cm.

◀ DOG COCKLE

Large, thick shell with brown markings. Burrows just below sand surface. 6.5cm.

➡ HEART COCKLE

Look at shell on its side to see heart shape. Lives in muddy sand below tide level but may be washed ashore. 9.5cm.

MOLLUSCS

◄ NECKLACE SHELL
Preys on other molluscs. Bores a neat hole in shells and eats flesh inside. On sandy shores. 3cm.

➡ WING OYSTER
Takes its name from its shape. Attached to stones in deeper waters of the Mediterranean and Atlantic. Uncommon. 7cm.

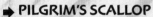

Rib

◄ COMMON WENTLETRAP
Look for raised ribs. Usually in deep water, sometimes on rocks on shore. Up to 4cm.

➡ PILGRIM'S SCALLOP
One of the biggest Mediterranean bivalves. Swims by clapping valves together. 13cm.

◄ MEDITERRANEAN TUN
Eats other molluscs. Deep water or washed ashore. 25cm.

➡ RAZOR SHELL
Uses its muscular foot to burrow up to 1m down in sand or mud. 15cm long.

⬅ SMOOTH VENUS
Pretty, shiny shell. Lives buried in sand or mud on all Mediterranean and some British shores. 11cm.

➡ BALTIC TELLIN
Burrows in mud and sand of sea and estuaries. 2cm.

⬅ ELEPHANT'S TUSK
Named for its shape. Lives in muddy sand of deeper water of Atlantic, English Channel and North Sea. 5cm long.

➡ TROUGH SHELL
Likes to burrow in clean sand or gravel of lower shores. Common. 5cm.

39

MOLLUSCS

← EDIBLE COCKLE
Very common. Burrows in sand
or mud from the lower
shore down. 5cm.

➡ SCREW SHELL
Long, thin shell, often found in large
numbers on sandy bottoms in deep
water. Empty shells are sometimes
washed ashore. 6cm.

← BANDED WEDGE SHELL
Named after band markings.
Burrows in the sand on the
shore and in the water.
Empty shells often found
on the beach. 3.5cm.

Band markings

➡ PELICAN'S FOOT
Its unusual shape
makes this shell easy to
spot. Large numbers
live together on all
kinds of seabed. 5.5cm.

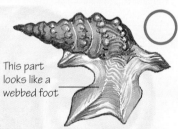

This part
looks like a
webbed foot

← COMMON SAND GAPER
So-called because the two
halves of the shell never
completely close. Lives in
sand and burrows deeper
as it grows bigger. 12cm.

➡ CHINK SHELL
Usually in shallow water, on seaweeds. Striped. 1cm.

◀ BLUE-RAYED LIMPET
Rows of blue spots are bright on young shells, faded on old ones. On brown seaweeds and holdfasts. 1.5cm.

➡ MEDITERRANEAN CONE
Do not touch. Has tooth filled with poison to catch prey. Mediterranean. Up to 5cm.

◀ HORSE MUSSEL
Usually on oarweed from lower shore to very deep water. One of Europe's largest mussels. Up to 20cm.

➡ FLAT PERIWINKLE
Can be brown, yellow, orange or striped. Feeds on wrack seaweeds. In rock pools. Common. 1cm.

◀ PHEASANT SHELL
Found mostly on red seaweeds in rock pools on lower shore. Small and glossy. 8mm.

SEA URCHINS AND STARFISH

These animals have prickly spines on their skin and rows of suckers which they use to pull themselves along and to hold onto rocks.

➡ BROWN SERPENT-STAR
Stripes on arms darken with age. Mediterranean. 10-15cm.

Spine

➡ COMMON MEDITERRANEAN SEA URCHIN
Holds bits of seaweed or shell over itself. Not in Britain. Up to 10cm.

⬇ BLACK SEA URCHIN
Black spines. Lower shore and deep water. Not in Britain. 6-10cm.

⬅ SMALL PURPLE-TIPPED SEA URCHIN
Spines have purple tips. Under rocks and stones on lower shore. Up to 4cm.

➡ EDIBLE SEA URCHIN
On rocky shores and offshore but becoming rare. Spines drop off when sea urchin dies. Shell is called a test. Up to 15cm.

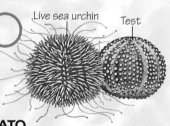

Live sea urchin

Test

⬅ SEA POTATO
Sea urchin which lives in sand at low tide level. Leaves a dent on surface where it has burrowed. Empty shells, called tests, may be washed ashore in storms. 5-6cm long.

Test

➡ SUNSTAR
Preys on other starfish. Spiny, with up to 15 arms. Often beautifully patterned. 4-8cm.

⬅ COMMON STARFISH
Five arms, like most starfish. Tips often turn up when starfish moves. Up to 50cm but those on shore only 5-10cm.

➡ MEDITERRANEAN MULTI-ARMED STARFISH
Six to eight arms, often of different lengths. 8-12cm.

⬅ CUSHION STARLET
Very small with short arms. Under rocks and in shady parts of rock pools. 1-2cm.

➡ SPINY STARFISH
Large spines. Colour varies. On lower shore and in deep water. 8-12cm.

➡ SMALL BRITTLE STAR
Very common but hard to spot. Under stones. 3cm.

➡ COMMON BRITTLE STAR
Very fragile, so handle gently. Under stones. 3-8cm.

Common brittle star

Small brittle star

CRUSTACEANS

This is a large group of animals which have shells to protect them.

Opening

◀ ACORN BARNACLE
Very common on rocks. Has a diamond-shaped opening in its shell for feeding. 1.5cm.

Opening

▶ STAR BARNACLE
Look on rocks. May be found near acorn barnacles. Opening is kite-shaped. 1.2cm.

Claw

◀ BEACH HOPPER
Jumps about when disturbed. Lives under stones and among seaweed high up on beach. Male has claws on second pair of legs. 2cm.

▶ SEA SCUD
Lives on muddy sand and in sheltered estuaries. Hides under stones on middle and lower shore. 1.3cm.

◀ GRIBBLE
Lives in wood. Look for the tiny holes it bores into piers and boat hulls. 4mm.

➡ SEA SLATER
Look in cracks in breakwaters and on rocks above high tide level. Moves down shore to feed as tide goes out. Runs fast. 2.5cm.

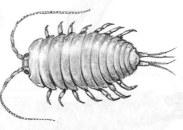

⬅ CHAMELEON PRAWN
Usually in deep water but may be found among seaweed in lower shore rock pools. Changes colour to match seaweed. 2.5cm.

➡ WHITE SHRIMP
Common in rock pools on lower shore and in shallow water in sandy estuaries. 5cm.

⬅ COMMON PRAWN
Common in shallow water, sometimes in rock pools. Like all prawns and shrimps, its feelers are longer than its body. 6.5cm.

Claw

➡ SAND SHRIMP
Common in sandy estuaries. Broad, flattened claws on first legs. 5cm.

Claw

CRUSTACEANS

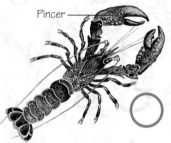

Pincer

◀ COMMON LOBSTER
Small ones sometimes found in lower shore rock pools. It is illegal to take any less than 8cm long. Strong pincers on front legs are slightly unequal. Up to 45cm.

➡ MONTAGU'S PLATED LOBSTER
Its last pair of legs may be hidden under its body. Under seaweed and stones. 4cm.

Claw

◀ BROAD-CLAWED PORCELAIN CRAB
Notice broad, hairy claws and very small back legs. Under stones on middle and lower shores. 1.2cm.

➡ LONG-CLAWED PORCELAIN CRAB
Long claws are not hairy. Can be found among stones and on oarweed holdfasts (see page 18). Lower shore. 1.2cm.

Shell of common whelk

◀ COMMON HERMIT CRAB
Has no hard shell of its own to protect its soft body, so lives in empty shells like this one. Found in rock pools. Up to 10cm.

➡ SPONGE CRAB

Covered in hairs and looks furry.
Often carries a piece of sponge
on its back, held by last two
pairs of legs. In rock pools.
Rare. 7cm.

Pincer

⬅ SHORE CRAB

Has broad, smooth shell.
Young ones often have
attractive markings.
Common on sandy
and rocky shores. 4cm.

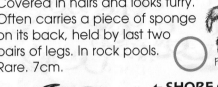

➡ VELVET SWIMMING CRAB

Has red eyes, with 8-10 small
points in between, on
shell edge. Hairy shell.
Lower shore and shallow
water. 8cm.

Broad back legs
act as swimming
paddles

⬅ PENNANT'S CRAB

Has long, smooth shell. Uses
its last pair of legs as
swimming paddles. Swims
near sandy bottom in
shallow water. Burrows
fast. 3.5cm.

➡ HAIRY CRAB

Has wide, hairy body and
unequal pincers. Common
in some places. Among
stones and seaweed
on lower shore. 2cm.

47

CRUSTACEANS

◀ FURROWED CRAB
Blunt teeth on edge of shell between the eyes. Found under large rocks and stones and among seaweed, on lower shore. 2.5cm.

➡ LESS FURROWED CRAB
Found under rocks and stones on lower shore. Sharper teeth on edge of shell. Hairy legs. Rare. 2cm.

◀ ROCK CRAB
Can stay out of water for a long time. Clings to rocks and can run fast. Common in Mediterranean. Not found in Britain. 3cm.

➡ EDIBLE CRAB
Large ones found in deep water, but small ones common in rock pools, under rocks and buried in sand on lower shore. Up to 11.5cm.

◀ TOOTHED PIRIMELA
Similar in shape to shore crab, but has larger teeth on shell edge, and front edge is more pointed. 1cm.

➡ THORNBACK SPIDER CRAB ◯

Shell is oval and spiny. Often caught in lobster pots. Sometimes in rock pools on lower shore, and in oarweed. 15cm.

Beak

⬅ SLENDER-LEGGED SPIDER CRAB

Notice long beak. Often has bits of seaweed or sponge on shell. Moves slowly. ◯ In rock pools. 1.8cm.

➡ TOAD CRAB ◯

Pear-shaped shell often covered with sponges and seaweed. Eyes can be withdrawn into sockets. In lower shore rock pools. 10cm.

Common mussel

⬅ PEA CRAB

Lives inside bivalve shells. Female is large and soft; male is ◯ small with hard shell. Up to 1.2cm.

JELLYFISH

These animals are not all real jellyfish, but are closely related. They swim by sucking water into their bodies, then jetting it out underneath. They catch prey with their tentacles.

Float

◄ PORTUGUESE MAN- O'-WAR
Made up of many tiny creatures, living as a colony. Floats on the sea, but sometimes washed ashore. Don't touch; tentacles sting. Float 15cm long.

Tentacle

➡ BY-THE-WIND SAILOR
May be blown ashore in winds. Sometimes in shoals. Harmless. 3cm.

◄ MOON JELLYFISH
Transparent with purple rim and crescents. Four tentacles under body. Very common. Harmless. Up to 15cm.

➡ AEQUOREA
Lives in open sea, but often washed up on the beach. Common in late summer. Harmless. Up to 15cm.

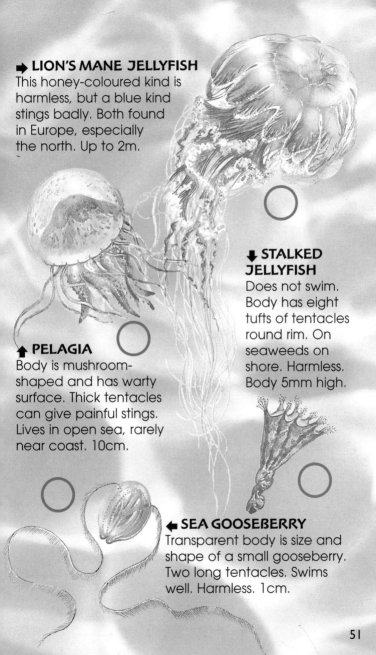

➡ LION'S MANE JELLYFISH
This honey-coloured kind is harmless, but a blue kind stings badly. Both found in Europe, especially the north. Up to 2m.

⬇ STALKED JELLYFISH
Does not swim. Body has eight tufts of tentacles round rim. On seaweeds on shore. Harmless. Body 5mm high.

⬆ PELAGIA
Body is mushroom-shaped and has warty surface. Thick tentacles can give painful stings. Lives in open sea, rarely near coast. 10cm.

⬅ SEA GOOSEBERRY
Transparent body is size and shape of a small gooseberry. Two long tentacles. Swims well. Harmless. 1cm.

WORMS

There are many kinds of worms which live on the shore. Some live in tubes of sand; others burrow in the sand or move on the surface.

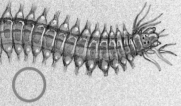

◀ RAGWORM
Has bristles along each side and a red line down its back. Burrows in sand and mud. From middle shore to shallow water. 10cm.

➡ LUGWORM
Fat worm with thin tail. Lives buried in sand. Wormcasts and hollows show where two ends of its burrow are (see page 55).15cm.

Gills for breathing

◀ SAND MASON
Long, thin worm that lives in a tube buried in the sand. Tip of tube, made of sand and shell bits, sticks up above surface. 20cm.

➡ KEELWORM
Worm lives in hard white tube which has a ridge along the top. Look on rocks, stones and empty shells. Up to 3cm.

Gill

◀ GREEN LEAF WORM
Crawls among barnacles and under seaweed on rocks, or hides in rock crevices. Upper shore to shallow water. 10cm.

SEA SLUGS

Sea slugs are molluscs that have no shells. They have tentacles on their heads and are often brightly coloured.

← GREEN SEA SLUG
Lives on seaweeds from middle shore down. Colour varies from green to bright red depending on what it feeds on. About 3cm.

Gills for breathing

→ SEA LEMON
Warty body with two tentacles and a ring of gills. Found among rocks in deep water, but comes ashore in summer to lay its eggs. 6cm.

← GREY SEA SLUG
One of the largest sea slugs in Europe. Common on rocky shores between tide marks, under stones. Feeds on sea anemones. Up to 8cm.

→ LIMACIA CLAVIGERA
Body usually white, with red-tipped fronds along its back. In shallow water. 2cm.

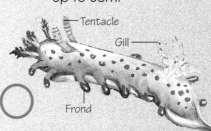

Tentacle

Gill

Frond

CUTTLEFISH, OCTOPUS, SQUID

These molluscs have large soft bodies and several "arms" or tentacles. They can change colour.

➡ **COMMON CUTTLEFISH**
Colour can change quickly when frightened. Internal shell, or cuttlebone, often washed ashore. In sheltered bays. Up to 30cm.

Cuttlebone

◀ **COMMON OCTOPUS**
Lives among rocks and oarweeds. Sometimes in rock pools. Uses tentacles to move about on sea bottom. Up to 1m.

➡ **COMMON SQUID**
Rarely found near shore but thick internal shell, or "pen", is sometimes washed up. Up to 60cm.

Pen

◀ **EUROPEAN FLYING SQUID**
Can sometimes be seen swimming near the surface of the sea at night. Up to 60cm.

MARKS IN THE SAND

A sandy beach may look empty, but look closely for signs like these left by seashore animals. Their tracks show up best in wet sand at low tide.

◄ Look for the pointed claws of gulls' tracks. The webbing shows only in soft, wet sand.

➡ The sand mason lives in the sand in a tube of shell bits. The fringed tip of the tube sticks up out of the sand.

◄ The sea potato leaves a dent in the sand where it burrows.

➡ A tern's tracks are small, with very narrow webbing.

Tail end of worm is under wormcast

Head end of worm is ——— under here

◄ Lugworms suck in sand and digest any edible scraps. Then they pass the sand out, leaving a wormcast on the surface.

USEFUL WORDS

air bladders – pockets filled with air, which help some seaweeds to float.

estuary – the place where a large river meets the sea; a river mouth.

fleshy – plump, thick (used to describe leaves).

frond – the leaf of a seaweed.

holdfast – a root-like structure at the base of seaweed stems, which anchors the seaweed to rocks.

marsh – an area of low-lying land which gets flooded either by a river or the sea.

offshore – out at sea, some way from a shore.

prey – an animal that is hunted by another animal for food.

saltmarsh – a marsh which gets flooded by sea water.

sand dunes – a mound or ridge of loose sand formed by the wind. Dunes often have plants growing on them.

school – a large number of fish or whales all swimming together.

shingle – pebbles which have been rounded and worn to roughly the same small size by the sea; a beach which is made up of these pebbles.

shoal – a large number of fish all swimming together.

spine – a stiff, sharp-pointed outgrowth on a plant or animal; a prickle.

tentacle – a thin, flexible "arm" which some animals use for grasping.

wormcast – a mass of sand or mud which is thrown up to the surface by a worm after it has passed through the worm's body.

WEß SITES TO VISIT

If you have access to the Internet, you will be able to find out more about seashore life on-line. Here are some Web sites to try.

British Marine Life Study Society – for detailed information on seashore life around Britain, including a section for 7-14 year-olds, with quizzes.
http://ourworld. compuserve.com/ homepages/BMLSS/

The Sea – for information about seas and sea life, games to play and links to conservation organizations.
http://www.seasky.org/sea. html

Marine Conservation Society – find out about pollution and conservation around the UK's seashores.
http://www.mcsuk.mcmail. com/

Ocean 98 – for facts and figures about seas and sea life around the world.
http://www.ocean98.org/

The Wildlife Trust – to get involved in wildlife conservation in the UK, you could join Wildlife Watch, a club for young environmentalists, with many local branches.
http://www.wildlifetrust. org.uk/

Naturenet – for lists of nature reserves in your area, including those at the coast, and for general information about nature conservation.
http://naturenet.net/

Royal Society for the Protection of Birds – find out which are good nature reserves for watching birds at the coast, and how to join the Young Ornithologists' Club.
http://rspb.org.uk/

Greenscreen – for general information about the environment specially written for young people by young people.
http://www.greenscreen. org/

SCORECARD

The animals and plants in this scorecard are in alphabetical order. When you spot a species, fill in the date next to its score. Rare species score more than common ones.

After a day's spotting, add up all the points you have scored on a sheet of paper and keep a note of them. See if you can score more points another day.

Name of species	Score	Date spotted	Name of species	Score	Date spotted
Acorn barnacle	5		Bryopsis	15	
Aequorea	20		Buckshorn plantain	10	
Annual seablite	15		Butterfish	10	
Avocet	20		By-the-wind sailor	25	
Baltic tellin	5		Chameleon prawn	10	
Banded wedge shell	10		Channelled wrack	5	
Beach hopper	5		Chink shell	10	
Beadlet anemone	5		Chough	25	
Bird's foot trefoil	10		Common brittle star	10	
Black sea urchin	15		Common cerith	25	
Black-headed gull	5		Common cuttlebone	5	
Bladder wrack	5		Common cuttlefish	25	
Blue-rayed limpet	15		Common dolphin	20	
Bottle-nosed dolphin	25		Common hermit crab	5	
Bread sponge	10		Common limpet	5	
Broad-clawed porcelain crab	10		Common lobster	25	
Brown serpent-star	10		Common Mediterranean sea urchin	10	

Name of species	Score	Date spotted	Name of species	Score	Date spotted
Common mussel	5		Dunlin	10	
Common octopus	25		Edible cockle	5	
Common oyster	5		Edible crab	10	
Common periwinkle	5		Edible sea urchin	10	
Common porpoise	25		Elephant's tusk	15	
Common prawn	5		European flying squid	25	
Common sand gaper	10		File shell	25	
Common seal	15		Flat periwinkle	5	
Common squid	25		Fool's cap	15	
Common starfish	10		Furrowed crab	20	
Common tern	10		Golden samphire	15	
Common wentletrap	15		Great black-backed gull	5	
Common whelk	5		Great topshell	15	
Corkwing wrasse	15		Green leaf worm	10	
Cormorant	10		Green sea slug	15	
Cup coral	25		Grey sea slug	10	
Curlew	10		Grey seal	15	
Cushion starlet	10		Gribble	20	
Dab	15		Guillemot	15	
Dahlia anemone	15		Gut laver	10	
Daisy anemone	20		Hairy crab	15	
Dead man's fingers	10		Haliclona oculata	15	
Dog cockle	10		Heart cockle	25	
Dog whelk	5		Hermit crab anemone	25	
Dove shell	25		Herring gull	5	

Name of species	Score	Date spotted	Name of species	Score	Date spotted
Horse mussel	10		Nun cowrie	15	
Irish moss	10		Oarweed	10	
Keelworm	5		Otter	25	
Knotted wrack	5		Oystercatcher	10	
Laver	10		Painted topshell	10	
Less furrowed crab	20		Pea crab	20	
Lesser black-backed gull	5		Pelagia	25	
Lesser rorqual	25		Pelican's foot	20	
Limacia clavigera	20		Pennant's crab	10	
Lion's mane jellyfish	25		Pheasant shell	20	
Little tern	20		Phymatolithon	15	
Long-clawed porcelain crab	10		Pilgrim's scallop	25	
Lugworm cast	5		Plocamium	15	
Lurid cowrie	25		Plumrose anemone	15	
Marram grass	10		Portuguese man-o'-war	20	
Mediterranean cone	25		Precious coral	25	
Mediterranean monk seal	25		Puffin	20	
Mediterranean multi-armed starfish	10		Ragworm	10	
Mediterranean tun	25		Rainbow wrasse	25	
Mermaid's cup	25		Razor shell	10	
Montagu's blenny	15		Razorbill	15	
Montagu's plated lobster	10		Redshank	10	
Moon jellyfish	5		Ringed plover	5	
Necklace shell	15		Rock crab	25	
Netted dog whelk	10		Rock dove	25	

Name of species	Score	Date spotted	Name of species	Score	Date spotted
Rock goby	10		Sea oak	15	
Saddle oyster	15		Sea orange	25	
Sand eel	15		Sea potato test	5	
Sand goby	5		Sea purslane	10	
Sand mason	10		Sea sandwort	10	
Sand shrimp	5		Sea scud	5	
Sand-smelt	15		Sea slater	10	
Sargasso weed	20		Sea stickleback	15	
Scorpion fish	25		Sea wormwood	15	
Screw shell	10		Shag	15	
Scypha ciliata	10		Shelduck	10	
Sea arrowgrass	10		Shore clingfish	25	
Sea aster	10		Shore crab	5	
Sea bindweed	10		Shore rockling	15	
Sea campion	5		Slender-legged spider crab	15	
Sea chain	25		Slipper limpet	5	
Sea fan	20		Small brittle star	10	
Sea gooseberry	20		Small purple-tipped sea urchin	10	
Sea holly	10		Smooth venus	20	
Sea kale	20		Snakelocks anemone	10	
Sea lavender	10		Spiny starfish	15	
Sea lemon	10		Sponge crab	25	
Sea lettuce	5		Stalked jellyfish	20	
Sea mayweed	10		Star barnacle	5	
Sea milkwort	10		Stargazer	25	

Name of species	Score	Date spotted	Name of species	Score	Date spotted
Sting winkle	20		Variegated scallop	15	
Sunstar	10		Velvet swimming crab	10	
Thick-lipped grey mullet	10		Wartlet anemone	20	
Thornback spider crab	10		Weever	20	
Thrift/Sea pink	5		White piddock	15	
Toad crab	10		White shrimp	5	
Tompot blenny	15		White-beaked dolphin	25	
Toothed pirimela	25		Wing oyster	20	
Trough shell	10		Worm pipefish	15	
Two-banded bream	25		Yellow horned poppy	15	

NOTES

INDEX